MAKE IT!
WRITE IT!
READ IT!

Simple Bookmaking Projects to Engage Kids in Art and Literacy

Wendy M. L. Libby

Zephyr Press

Chicago

Published by Zephyr Press
An imprint of Chicago Review Press Incorporated
814 North Franklin Street
Chicago, Illinois 60610
ISBN 978-1-61373-030-0

Library of Congress Cataloging-in-Publication Data
Libby, Wendy M. L.
Make it! Write it! Read it! : simple bookmaking projects to engage kids in art and literacy / Wendy M.L. Libby. — First edition.
        pages cm
Summary: "Develops both art and literacy skills through the craft of bookmaking, inspiring elementary-aged children to read, write, and tell stories with their creations. Creative, fun, field-tested projects for teachers, parents, counselors, or other caregivers to work through with children ages 3–8 include 17 different blank book designs. These designs are then applied to 23 specific book projects"—Provided by publisher.
Includes bibliographical references and index.
ISBN 978-1-61373-030-0 (paperback)
1. Book design—Study and teaching (Elementary) 2. Bookbinding—Study and teaching (Elementary) 3. Art—Study and teaching (Elementary)—Activity programs. 4. Language arts (Elementary)—Activity programs. 5. Literacy—Study and teaching (Elementary) I. Title.
Z246.L675 2015
372.5´2044—dc23

2014036120

Cover and interior design: Monica Baziuk
Cover and interior photographs: Wendy M. L. Libby
Interior Illustrations: Jim Spence

Printed in the United States of America
5 4 3 2 1

To my husband, Bob,
and my sons,
Brandon and Bradley,
who believe in the power of creativity
and whose love and support
I could not do without.

A tiny egg is laid on a milkweed leaf.

A caterpillar eats away at the milkweed leaf.

A chrysalis forms around the caterpillar allowing a butterfly to grow inside.

After the wings dry the butterfly flutters in the sky.

Contents

PART 2
BOOKMAKING PROJECTS 39

MAKE IT!
WRITE IT!
READ IT!

Introduction

MAKING ART AND telling stories are two basic means of self-expression and self-development in all cultures. They both require planning, developing, and organizing thoughts. Creating art develops social, emotional, cognitive, sensory, and motor skills. Art activities can provide abundant learning experiences for a child. Effective learning takes place when an art activity reinforces lessons with hands-on experiences. Facilitating learning and development in children requires creativity—learning should be entertaining and something they enjoy. Children learn through experience, and art is an experience that involves independent thinking, exploration, problem solving, creativity, and free expression. Many literacy-rich activities can be brought to a child through art.

A toddler will scribble long before he or she has the ability to write. For the young child, these scribbles are a way to explore cause and effect and to work on developing fine motor skills and eye-hand coordination. As they use these new skills to create projects, children begin to use art and literacy together, and learning becomes more personal and engaging. Using visual arts can also generate lively discussions. Children become enthusiastic and excited about their world through stories and illustrations, and they can reply creatively through art experiences. Connecting art and literacy allows children to practice creativity while discovering a meaningful way to use language arts.

One way to make this connection is to use storybooks. After reading a book a child can integrate the story into his or her own experiences by creating an art activity based on the story or illustrations. Stories can coincide with a child's interest or an area of classroom study. For example, in the spring when insects are out and about, children can read a book about bugs and look at the illustrations to spark conversation. Children can re-create a real insect or make an imaginary one by drawing, painting, cutting and pasting, or molding one with clay or even constructing one with recycled materials. When their bug is completed they can then tell or write a story about their creation, such as where it might live, what it might eat, or how it became their friend. These activities make connections between books and art as well as between new reading experiences and real life. Asking open-ended questions about their art projects helps children discover connections between what they read and what they are creating and keeps them interested and engaged.

Art and literacy activities develop skills and competencies through creative and intuitive thinking. They contribute to seeing more, recalling more, and expressing with more confidence. Problem-solving skills, motivation, and self-discipline increase, and concentration develops.

As children create, they begin linking words to their discoveries. Pictures develop into stories with descriptions, sounds, feelings, and meanings. The art of making books allows children to personally connect with their own stories and get excited about creative expression, the art of handcrafting something, and writing simple stories. Children will enjoy sharing their work and rereading their books over and over—to themselves and to others—thereby sparking a love for books that can last a lifetime.

Nurturing Creativity

Before starting an art and writing activity, use descriptive games to inspire and nurture creativity. Focus on using the five senses—seeing, hearing, feeling, tasting, and smelling—to develop and strengthen project ideas. For example, ask a child to list five things that describe how a puppy feels, or ask which he or she can picture better: a bowl of ice cream or a bowl of creamy vanilla ice cream that has swirls of chocolate, is smothered in hot fudge, and is topped with whipped cream, crunchy cashew nuts, colored sprinkles, and a round, sweet, red cherry?

Encourage children to act like detectives. Detectives do not miss anything. They do not notice just that it is raining but also that the raindrops make a pattern on the windowpane when they drip from the roof. Children's knowledge and productivity are strengthened when they learn how to see and how to respond to what they see. Use visuals to encourage more critical verbal interpretation and higher-quality communication. Pictures lead to words, and words reveal meanings, adding to the power behind the pictures.

The combination of art and literacy inspires both reading pictures and picturing writing. Reading pictures means viewing, discussing, and interpreting artworks. It helps students develop ideas for projects from their own perspectives. Often the art reminds them of personal things. The steps to reading a picture involve describing, analyzing, interpreting, and evaluating. Describing is the *what*, the visual information. Analyzing is the *how*, what the artist did with the elements and principles. Interpreting is the *why*, speculating and giving meaning. Evaluating means making a judgment, not just stating one's personal preference but judging whether the artist has expressed what he or she intended. Encouraging children to analyze what they see helps them develop their imaginations, critical-thinking skills, and powers of observation.

Picturing writing involves creating an artwork and then reflecting on it through written word. Most adults will ask a child to write a story and then illustrate it when they should be asking a child to illustrate his or her thoughts and then write the story. This process helps the child organize thoughts more freely with more detail.

Parents, teachers, and other adults can create a stimulating atmosphere for art and literacy learning by creating a rich environment full of books, art, writing, and print materials. Plan field trips to art museums and studios, libraries, and performances that allow children to gain real-world experiences. Provide visual stimulation with artwork, pictures, reproductions, photos, and books. Tell stories and sing songs.

Differential Learning

Differentiation recognizes individual differences in learners. Developing instructional differentiation requires building a curriculum that considers the needs, preferences, and diversities of all children and provides learning experiences with options for content, process, and/or products. Through art and literacy activities, children with different learning styles have options of how to communicate their ideas and express their knowledge. Students are able to demonstrate their learning as well as apply and extend their knowledge through bookmaking activities.

Art is a perfect place for differentiated instruction. All children, including those with physical, emotional, or academic limitations, can create and find success through art. As a visual language, art allows ESL and non-English-speaking children the opportunity to participate in learning. Multiple modes of learning take place through art and present opportunities to reach each and every child as well as to connect learning across the school curriculum.

Art allows for open-ended activities that permit children to work at their own levels of ability. Some might be able to skillfully create their work but with little imagination. Others might be able to express with their imagination but have little control of manipulative skills. Whether considered a struggling learner, an average learner, or a gifted learner, a child can be challenged to be creative. Support for those who may struggle with their attempts. Ask leading questions such as: "What do you think should be done next?" "What would you like to do now?" and "What can you add to this?" Encourage gifted students to use the high-order thinking skills of analysis, synthesis, and evaluation. The activities in this book can be tailored to all learners for differentiated instruction. The directions for the bookmaking activities are basic guidelines and can be altered accordingly by simplifying or expanding them as needed.

Literacy Connection

From birth, children participate in a variety of language and literacy activities. Young children enjoy hearing books read to them before they learn to read independently. Reading aloud to children exposes them to vocabulary and piques interest. The term *emergent* refers to an evolving and developing understanding. It identifies the early stages of literacy, when a child participates in pretend reading and scribble writing, which are recognized as essential developmental steps to becoming fluent readers and writers.

Reading is a basis for all other academic skills, and bookmaking activities help make learning to read meaningful and enjoyable. The written text of the books can be shared writing, where the adult and child compose the text together; guided writing, where the adult supports strategies and skills of the child; or independent writing, where children choose their own topics and write independently.

The very young can work with wordless picture books by creating illustrations to tell their stories. They can label their pictures or write one-word descriptions or thoughts to begin the process of developing literacy. Older children will be able to make and illustrate their own books and then compose words, sentences, poems or stories to fit the illustrations. Depending on age, skill, and interest in poetry or prose, various literacy genres can be adapted to the crafted books. Children can employ poetic forms of verse, such as acrostic, cinquain, and limerick, or embrace narratives of fiction or nonfiction such as fables, fairy tales, myths, stories, biographies, science fiction, and informational books.

How to Use This Book

The projects in this book guide children to make their own books that they then fill with their own stories. The first section shows how to make several blank books, which children can use for writing or drawing simple stories of their choice or about a given subject matter or theme. Many different types of books are included, such as an accordion-fold book and a pop-up book.

The second section provides directions for making specific books using the blank books. Although specific themes and materials are given, they are merely suggestions. They are ones that I have personally used with children. The bookmaking activities included in this book can always be used with other motivational themes or curriculum studies.

As an art teacher I have based these lessons around art elements and principles which I list at the beginning of each activity. The elements of art or design are what an artist uses to create a work of art. These include line, shape, color, texture, value, form, and space. The principles of art or design are how an artist uses the elements. Art principles consist of balance, contrast, emphasis, movement, pattern, rhythm, and unity. Materials lists are provided for each project; however, materials can be added, deleted, or changed for more open-ended projects. The directions provide sequential steps to follow yet leave room for creativity. I suggest being flexible and allowing children the freedom to be inspired and inventive. The instructional portion of the activity is left up to the adult who will gear the verbal or written part of the book to the literary concepts and objectives of a child's particular level. The text written in the constructed book can be as creative and as engaging as the bookmaking activity, whether writing fiction or nonfiction, story or poetry.

The very young child can illustrate books in a variety of ways using his or her own creative way of manipulating art materials. An adult can help prepare materials and facilitate activities. For example, a preschool child can look for pictures in old magazines and have an adult assist in cutting them out, gluing them onto blank book pages, and connecting the pictures and words. The adult can just listen to the story as the child reads the pictures or he or she can write down what the child says and then read the book back to the child. Or, an adult can assist in labeling the pictures with words. This helps the child in making connections between the drawings and the written word. Older children will be able to make and illustrate their own books and then write sentences, stories, poems, or descriptions, depending on the literary concept. In the end, the important result is that the child has helped create a book with personal connections that will spark storytelling.

PART I

BLANK BOOK PROJECTS

CHILDREN CAN MAKE many different types of books with a few simple directions and materials. The blank books they learn how to make here by following the step-by-step instructions can then be used to make their own creative book. The folding and assembling techniques presented in this section will be referred to in the specific bookmaking activities in Part II.

Each of these projects can be modified to fit your needs. For example, a certain size paper or amount of pages might be listed in the directions, but those details can be altered. The most common materials for these projects are papers, card stock, scissors, glue, a stapler, a pencil, colored pencils, markers, and crayons. The projects are arranged in order of increasing difficulty, starting with a simple folded piece of paper and culminating in a stitched book with decorative covers and endpapers.

Simple Book

Materials

- 3 to 5 pieces of white paper, 8½ by 11 inches
- 1 piece of colored construction paper or card stock, 8½ by 11 inches
- String, yarn, or ribbon, 24 inches long

Directions

➜ Fold each piece of white paper in half, short edge to short edge.

➜ Open the folds and stack the papers on top of each other.

➜ Refold the papers all together.

➜ Make a cover from the colored construction paper or card stock by folding it, short edge to short edge, and tucking the folded pages into the crease. The cover can be the same size or slightly larger than the pages.

➜ Wrap the string, yarn, or ribbon around all the pages and the cover at the fold, and tie into a bow or knot.

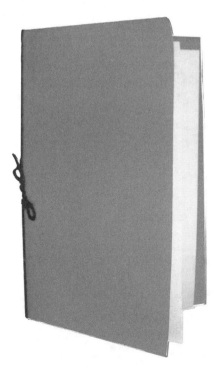

Flip Book

Materials

- 10 or more pieces of white paper, 3 by 4 inches
- 1 piece of colored construction paper, 1 by 3 inches
- Stapler

Directions

➜ Stack the sheets of white paper on top of each other. Flip books work best when the pages are small, because they are easier to flip. For best results there should be at least ten pages for flipping.

➜ Make a spine by folding the colored construction paper in half, long edge to long edge.

➜ Sandwich the pages inside the spine and staple through the spine and the pages near the top and near the bottom.

Half-Cover Book

Materials

- 1 piece of colored construction paper, 9 by 12 inches
- Scissors
- 3 to 5 pieces of white paper, 3½ by 5 inches
- 3 to 5 pieces of colored construction paper, 4 by 5½ inches
- Glue
- Stapler

Directions

➤ Lay the large sheet of colored construction paper in front of you, horizontally.

➤ Fold the paper in half, short edge to short edge.

➤ Open the front cover, and find the middle of the front short edge. From the edge to the fold, cut the front cover in half. You may cut on either a straight or wavy line.

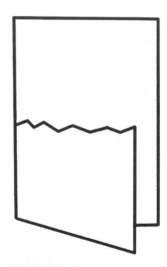

➤ On the fold, cut down from the top of the cover to the first cut. Remove the top half of the front cover.

➤ Glue the white papers to the small colored construction papers to make your interior pages.

➤ Staple the stack of pages to the inside of the folded book, below the remaining front-cover flap.

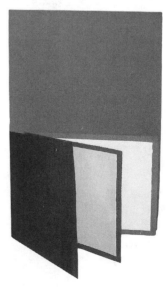

Accordion-Fold Book

Materials

- 1 piece of white paper, 11 by 17 inches
- 2 pieces of colored construction paper or card stock, 8½ by 11 inches
- Glue

Directions

→ Fold the white piece of paper in half, short edge to short edge.

→ Open the paper back up, and on one side of the crease, fold the paper in half again.

→ Repeat this folding step on the other side of the crease.

→ On the middle crease, fold the right half underneath the left half to make a zigzag.

→ Optional: It is also possible to use more than one sheet of paper. After folding them in the zigzag style, glue the back

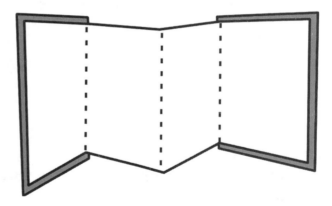

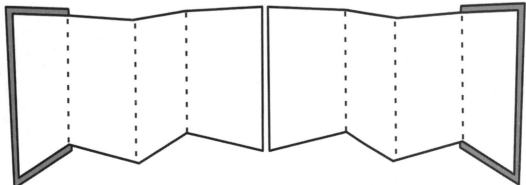

of the end piece of one folded section to the front piece of another folded paper.

➜ Glue the colored construction paper or card stock to each end to make the covers.

Coffee-Filter Pockets Book

Materials

- 3 to 5 large cone coffee filters
- 3 to 5 small cone coffee filters
- Glue
- Stapler

Directions

➜ Center a small filter on top of a large filter to create a page.

➜ Glue it down, and repeat for all other small filters.

➜ Stack all the large filters in a pile and staple along the left edge.

➜ The open tops of the filters become pockets into which you can place your writing.

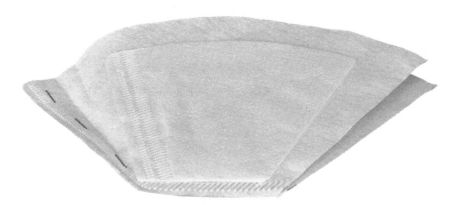

Materials

- 1 rectangular piece of paper
- Scissors

Directions

➡ Fold the paper in half, long edge to long edge.

➡ Fold the paper again, short edge to short edge.

➡ Fold short edge to short edge one more time.

➡ Open the paper completely.

➡ Refold once, short edge to short edge. There will be four rectangle shapes on each half, formed by the creases. Leave the paper folded.

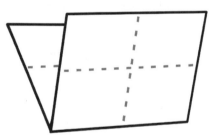

➡ Locate the crease that extends from the side fold across the middle of the paper.

➡ Cut on the folded line in the middle of the paper from the folded edge to the point where the corners from all four rectangles meet in the middle. Do not cut all the way to the edge of the paper.

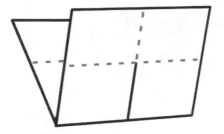

➜ Unfold the paper and refold it long edge to long edge. Holding the end rectangles together, push the two ends slowly toward the middle until the middle rectangles open outward.

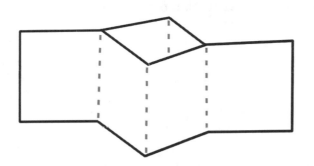

➜ Push the two end rectangles completely together until they touch. Fold all the papers flat so that only two rectangles are showing.

➜ Fold the book closed along the middle crease. Now you have a little book with a front and back cover and six pages.

Three-Part Section Book

Materials

- 3 pieces of white paper, 6 by 12 inches
- 1 piece of colored construction paper, 2 by 12 inches
- Stapler
- Ruler
- Pencil
- Scissors

Directions

➡ Stack the three white papers together with the long edge on the top and bottom.

➡ Fold the colored construction paper in half, long edge to long edge. This will be your book's spine, which holds the pages together.

➡ Sandwich the three papers together inside the folded spine piece. Staple the sandwich together, once at each end and once in the middle of the strip.

➡ Place the book in front of you with the spine at the top, horizontally. From one end, measure 4 inches and make a small mark with a pencil. Make another small mark at 8 inches.

→ At each mark, use your scissors to cut the pages from the bottom of the pages up to the spine, equally dividing the book into thirds. Do not cut through the colored spine paper.

Portfolio Book

Materials

- 2 pieces of colored construction paper, 9 by 12 inches
- 3 pieces of white paper, 4 by 8 inches
- strip of colored construction paper, ½ by 4 inches
- Ruler
- Scissors
- Stapler
- Glue
- Hole punch
- 2 brad fasteners
- String or yarn

Directions

➡ Lay one piece of colored construction paper in front of you, horizontally. Fold both short edges so that they meet in the middle.

➡ Open the side flaps.

➡ Stack the white pages on the middle section, centering them. Staple them along the top edge.

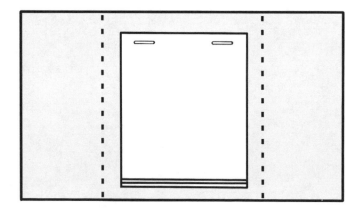

→ Glue the colored construction paper strip over the top edge to hide the staples.

→ Fold the two side pieces in to close the book.

→ Measure the side pieces from top to bottom, and mark the middle of the page along each center edge, about 1 inch in from where they meet.

→ Use the hole punch to make a hole at the mark on each cover. Put a brad fastener through each hole. Wrap the string or yarn around one fastener securely.

→ To close the book, fold the pages in and loosely wrap the string or yarn around the other fastener.

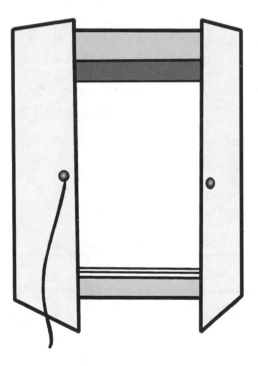

Shaped Subject Book

Materials

- 2 pieces of card stock
- Pencil
- Scissors
- 3 to 5 pieces of white paper
- Stapler

Directions

➔ On one piece of card stock, draw a picture of a theme for your book, such as an apple, a butterfly, or a house. This will be the front cover.

➔ Stack the two pieces of card stock and cut out the shape drawn. This will give you a back cover the same shape as your front cover.

➔ Stack the sheets of white paper together.

➔ Use one piece of the cut card stock to trace the shape onto the top of the white paper stack.

→ Cut out the shape on the white paper stack, cutting a little inside the traced line to make the interior pages a little bit smaller than the covers.

→ Stack the white pages inside the card stock covers and staple them all together, either at the top or left-hand side.

One-Fold Pop-Up Book

Materials

- 1 piece of card stock, 6 by 9 inches
- Ruler
- Pencil
- Scissors

Directions

➜ Fold the card stock in half, short edge to short edge.

➜ Make a small mark on the fold 2½ inches from each edge.

➜ From each mark on the folded edge, make a 1½-inch cut toward the open side of the paper.

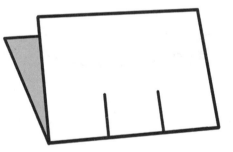

➜ Unfold the paper and pull the cut piece upward. Refold this piece on its crease, reversing the direction it folds.

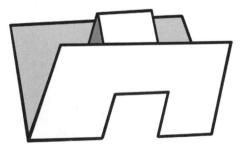

→ The fold will be the top edge for this book. Each time the page is opened, the small piece will pop up.

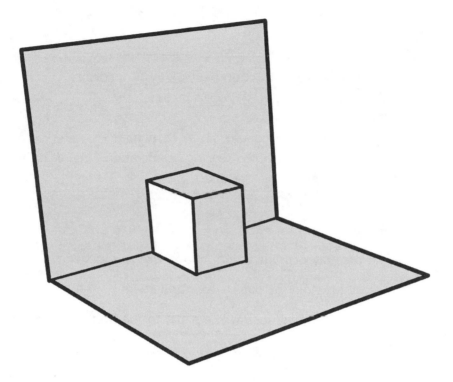

Double-Sided Book

Materials

- 1 piece of gray construction paper, 8 by 18 inches
- 1 piece of white paper, 5½ by 7½ inches
- Glue
- 3 to 5 pieces of white paper, 7½ by 11 inches
- Long stapler or long-eyed sewing needle and 15 inches of heavy thread or dental floss (optional)

Directions

→ Fold the gray paper in thirds, short edge to short edge.

→ Open and refold the paper accordion-style.

→ Glue the 5½-by-7½-inch white paper to the front fold for the cover.

→ Fold the pieces of larger white paper in half, short edge to short edge.

→ In the second fold, glue, staple, or stitch (using directions for the Stitched Book [page 35]) the folded white paper. These pages will appear to be in the back of the book.

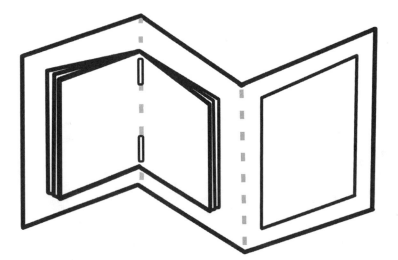

Paper-Bag Pockets Book

Materials

- 3 to 5 paper lunch bags (10¾ or 14 inches)
- Scissors
- Decorative paper (colored construction paper, wallpaper, wrapping paper, scrapbook paper, etc.)
- 2-inch strip of construction paper (5 or 6½ inches)
- Glue
- Colored paper
- Stapler

Directions

➜ Cut the bottom off the paper bags so the bag becomes a square. If using a 5-by-10¾-inch bag, the piece will measure 5 by 5 inches after cutting off the bottom. A 6½-by-14-inch bag will give you a 6½-inch square.

➜ Cut the decorative paper to the size of the square bag piece for as many bags as you are using for the book pages.

➜ Glue the decorative paper squares to the bags.

➜ Fold the colored construction paper in half, long edge to long edge, to make the book's spine.

→ Stack all the bag pages on top of each other with the cut edges to the same side and staple along the cut edge.

→ Put this edge into the fold of the colored paper and glue the spine over the stapled edge.

Folded-Pockets Book

Materials

- 1 piece of white paper, 9 by 18 inches
- Glue
- 4-by-6-inch index cards or heavy paper, such as colored construction paper or card stock

Directions

→ Place the piece of white paper in front of you horizontally, with the long sides of the paper serving as the top and bottom.

→ Fold the bottom edge up 2 inches.

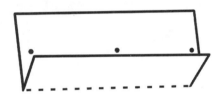

→ Put a small dot of glue on the outside corners of the fold to hold it in place.

→ Fold the paper in half short edge to short edge, and then again short edge to short edge.

→ Open and refold the paper accordion-style.

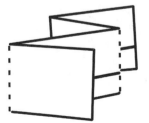

➡ Slide the 4-by-6-inch index cards or heavy paper into the pockets for pages.

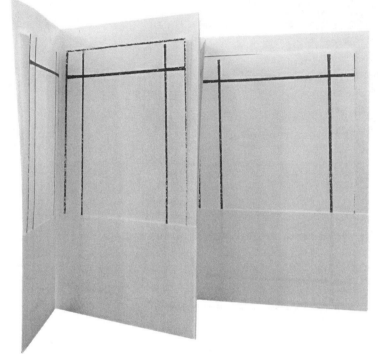

Hanging Tassel Book

Materials

- 4 pieces of white paper, 2½ by 5½ inches
- 4 pieces of colored card stock, 3 by 6 inches
- Glue
- Scissors
- String, yarn, or ribbon
- Beads (optional)

Directions

➡ Glue the four pieces of white paper to the four pieces of card stock.

➡ Fold each of the four pieces in half, short edge to short edge.

➡ Glue the back side of one half of one folded piece to the back side of half of another folded piece.

➡ Continue gluing half of one piece to half of another piece until the last half on the last piece of card stock is glued to the unglued half of the first piece.

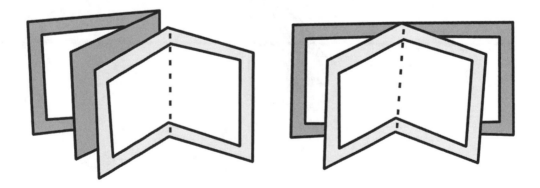

→ Fold the string, yarn, or ribbon in half and tie a loop at the folded end.

→ Lay one side of the string in the crease of one side. Lay the other side in the crease opposite the first one.

→ Tie the two string tails together just underneath the book. Allow the ends of the strands to hang down.

→ Add beads for decoration, if you like.

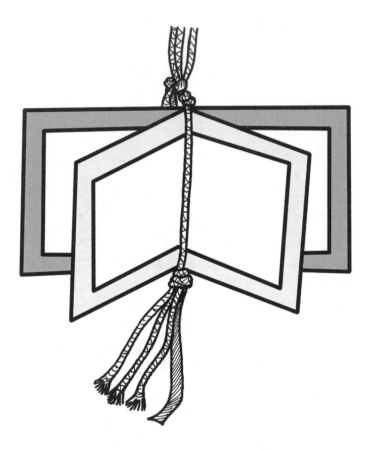

Tunnel Book

Materials

- 3 pieces of card stock, 5 by 6 inches
- Ruler
- Pencil
- Drawing compass
- Eraser
- Scissors
- 1 piece of card stock, 2 by 4 inches
- 2 pieces of white paper, 5 by 12 inches
- Glue

Directions

➜ Find the center of each edge of one piece of 5-by-6-inch card stock. Mark it on each side.

➜ Lightly draw a line to find where the lines intersect in the middle of the card stock.

➜ Open a compass to obtain a 1-inch radius.

➜ Place the point of the compass on the center of the paper, where the lines intersected, and draw a 2-inch-diameter circle.

➜ Erase the lines outside of the circle.

➜ Carefully poke the compass point tip through the center of the paper.

➜ Insert scissors, and cut out the circle. This is the front cover.

➜ Place the 2-by-4-inch card stock template on another piece of 5-by-6-inch card stock horizontally, and center it.

➜ Trace around the template.

➜ Carefully poke a hole in the middle of the rectangle, and cut it out from the card stock. Do not start cutting from the edge of the paper. This page eventually goes in the middle.

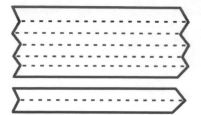

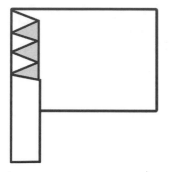

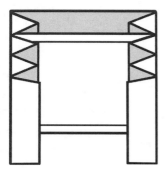

➜ Fold each piece of 5-by-12-inch paper in half, short edge to short edge. Fold one short edge up to the middle of the folded section. Fold it once more to bring the short edges together. Unfold the paper and refold accordion-style.

➜ To make the back cover, insert the uncut piece of 5-by-6-inch card stock into the last crease of the accordion-folded paper. Glue the last folded section to the back of the uncut card stock rectangle, along the short edge.

➜ Glue the last folded section of the other accordion-folded paper to the back side of the other short edge of the uncut rectangle.

➜ Glue the card stock with the rectangle cut out to the middle fold of each strip along the short edges of the card stock.

➜ Glue the card stock with the circle cut out to the first fold of each accordion-folded paper along the short edges.

Flap Book

Materials

- 1 piece of colored construction paper, 5 by 9 inches
- Glue
- 2 pieces of colored card stock, 3 by 9 inches
- 12 pieces of card stock, 2 by 3 inches

Directions

➜ Fold the colored construction paper long edge to long edge. Fold again long edge to long edge and then again one more time. Open the paper and refold it accordion-style along the creases.

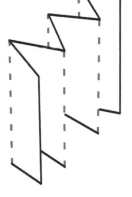

➜ Place the accordion in front of you, with the creases running vertically.

➜ Run a line of glue down the first rectangle on the left side of the accordion. Place one piece of 3-by-9-inch card stock into this first fold. The top flap of the accordion will be on the outside of your front cover.

➜ Repeat this step on the right side of the accordion with the other piece of 3-by-9-inch card stock. This becomes your back cover.

➤ Now take a piece of 2-by-3-inch card stock and put glue along the 2-inch edge. Stick the rectangle to the left side of the first fold, close to the top. The tag will stick out beyond the folded paper.

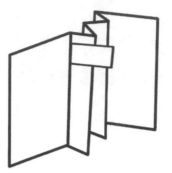

➤ Glue a second rectangle to the right side of the first fold, just below the first piece.

➤ Glue a third rectangle to the left of the first fold again and a fourth on the right. Each piece should be just below the previous piece.

➤ Repeat these steps, gluing four rectangles each to the next two folds.

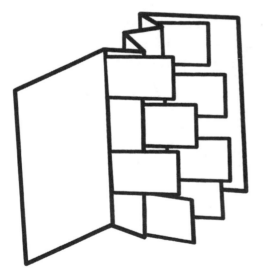

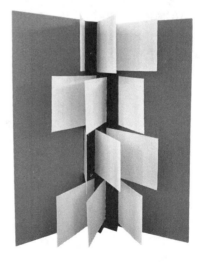

Pop-Up Book

Materials

- 1 piece of white paper, 8½ by 14 inches
- 2 pieces of colored card stock, 3½ by 8½ inches
- Glue
- 2 pieces of colored construction paper, 4 by 4 inches
- Scissors

Directions

➤ Fold the white paper in half, short edge to short edge, and in half again. Open the paper back up and refold accordion-style.

➤ Glue the colored card stock to the end pieces for the covers. The accordion flaps will make the inside front and back covers.

➤ To make the pop-up paper, fold a 4-by-4-inch colored construction paper in half. Open the paper and fold in half the other way.

➤ With the paper folded once, cut along the crease line from the center fold until ¼ inch from the edge of the paper.

➤ Keep the paper folded. From the fold, fold the two middle pieces along the cut toward the corners to create triangle folds. Crease well for a smooth edge.

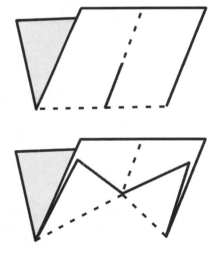

➜ Undo the triangle folds, push them to the inside, and press flat.

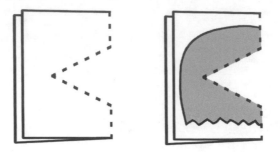

➜ Optional: Cut the edges of the paper to make various shapes for heads being careful not to cut the folded triangles. Leave enough paper arouond the edges to be able to glue it down.

➜ Repeat the steps to make another pop-up piece of paper with the other 4-inch square of colored construction paper.

➜ To assemble the pop-up in the book, align the center crease line of the pop-up with the first crease in the book. Glue the edges of the pop-up paper to the page. Repeat with the second pop-up paper, with its crease aligned with the third crease in the book.

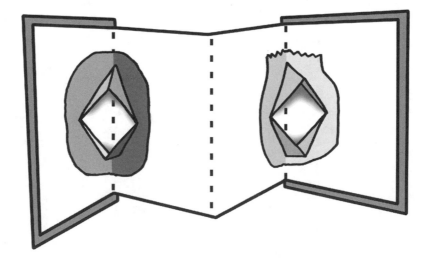

Mix-and-Match Book

Materials

- 1 piece of white paper, 6 by 12 inches
- 2 pieces of white paper, 6 by 6 inches
- Scissors
- Glue

Directions

→ Fold the 6-by-12-inch white paper in half, short edge to short edge.

→ Fold each piece of 6-by-6-inch white paper in half one way, and then in half the other way.

→ Open the square papers back up. Cut along the creases of one of the four folded square sections. These little squares will not be used and can be discarded.

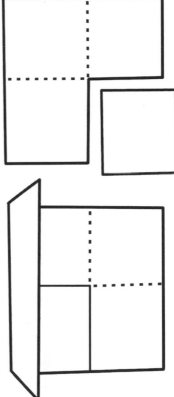

→ Open the 6-by-12-inch paper. This is going to be the cover of your book. On the right-hand side of the open cover, position one piece of the three-square papers so the cut-away square is at the bottom left. Glue the upper right corner of this page to the upper right corner of the cover paper. Only the top right square should be glued down. The other two squares should be left free to fold up and down or over.

→ With all the squares open and lying flat, position the other three-square paper with the cut-away square to the upper right corner. The bottom left corner will be on top of the cut-out area of the first paper. Glue this second page down in the left corner.

→ The small folded sections that are not glued down should open and close around each other, making many variations for the layout of the page.

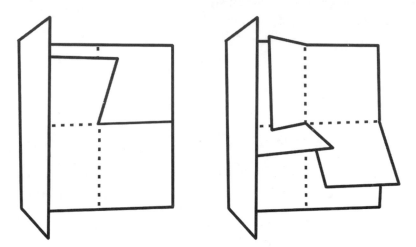

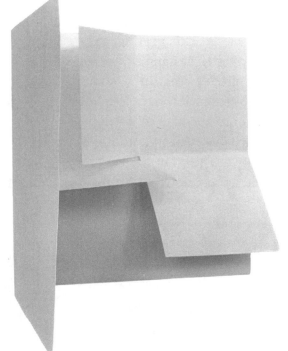

Three-Cover Book

Materials

- 3 pieces of decorative paper (colored construction paper, wallpaper, wrapping paper, scrapbook paper, etc.), 6 inches square
- 3 pieces of cardboard, 5 inches square
- Glue
- 1 piece of colored paper, 4½ by 15 inches
- 3 pieces of white paper, 4 by 8 inches
- Scissors
- Long-eyed sewing needle
- String, yarn, or ribbon

Directions

➔ Take a piece of decorative paper and cover the back side with glue.

➔ Place one of the cardboard pieces in the middle of the piece of decorative paper.

➔ Fold each corner of the paper in, and then fold in each side. Press the paper tightly around the cardboard.

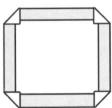

➔ Repeat with the other two pieces of decorative paper and cardboard squares.

➔ Fold the piece of colored paper into three equal parts. Open it back up. There will be three equal squares created by the creases.

➔ Spread glue on the bare, unpapered side of a cardboard square. Place it in the center of a square created by the creases in the colored paper.

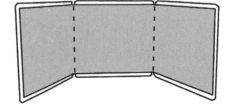

➔ Repeat with the other two cardboard squares.

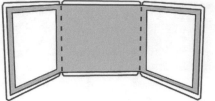

➜ Cut one piece of 4-by-8-inch paper in half. Glue one 4-by-4-inch piece onto each end of the colored paper, leaving the middle empty at this time. Set this assembly aside.

➜ Stack two pieces of 4-by-8-inch paper together and fold them in half.

➜ Using a long-eyed sewing needle, poke two holes, equally spaced, just below the fold. Thread a thin piece of string, yarn, or ribbon through the holes and make a bow.

➜ With the bow on the top edge, tear the top three pieces of paper across the bottom to make graduating lengths from shortest on the top to the longest on the bottom.

➜ Glue the untorn back page to the middle section of the book assembly. The bow should be at the top.

➜ To close the book, fold the two end covers over each other into the middle.

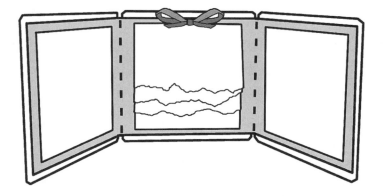

Stitched Book

Adult supervision required

Materials

- 3 to 5 pieces of white paper, 8½ by 11 inches
- 1 piece of colored paper, 8½ by 11 inches
- Pencil
- Long-eyed sewing needle
- Heavy thread or dental floss
- 2 pieces of cardboard, 6½ by 9½ inches
- 2 pieces of decorative paper (colored construction paper, wallpaper, wrapping paper, scrapbook paper, etc.), 8½ by 11 inches
- Glue
- Book tape or electrical tape

Directions

→ Fold the white papers in half, short edge to short edge. Open the papers and stack them together horizontally, with the long edges on top and bottom.

→ Fold the colored piece of paper, then open it, and place it on the bottom of the stack of white pages. This page will turn into the book's endpapers.

→ On the top sheet of white paper, mark a dot in the center of the fold. In all, you will make five small dots. They should be equally spaced. Start with the dot in the middle, and space two dots above and two dots below the middle dot.

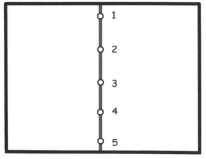

An adult will have to help young children with this and the next few steps.

→ Holding all pages open and together, poke the needle through the marked dots to make holes.

→ Thread the needle with heavy thread or dental floss, and make a knot on the bottom end of the thread. In the next steps you will be "back stitching," as in embroidery.

→ Poke the threaded needle through the middle hole (3) from the back or underneath side of the paper and pull through, leaving a couple of inches hanging.

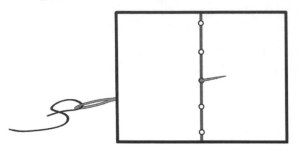

→ Poke the needle and thread down from the top side of the paper into the small hole directly above the middle hole (2), and pull the thread through.

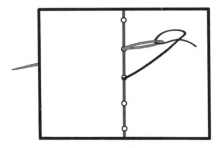

→ From the backside, stitch up through the top hole (1), and pull the thread through. Go back down through the hole directly below (2).

→ Skip the middle hole, and stitch up through the one right below it (4). Stitch down through the bottom hole (5).

→ Come back up through the hole right above (4), and then finally go down the middle hole (3). Knot the string ends together and cut the string, leaving about 1 inch.

→ To make the covers, take the two pieces of cardboard and glue the decorative paper to one side each, leaving an equal amount of paper all around the edges. Fold in the corners first, then all four sides, and glue them down.

→ Glue the outer colored paper from the stitched pages to the uncovered side of the cardboard covers.

→ Use a piece of book tape or electrical tape to connect the two cardboard pieces together at the center fold for the spine.

PART 2

BOOKMAKING PROJECTS

THIS SECTION GIVES directions for making specific books using the previous blank book designs. These projects connect to various educational topics and interests. Older children will be able to follow the directions on their own, whereas younger children will need some assistance in setup.

All children will be able to work independently on decoration, manipulation of materials, and creative choices. I suggest demonstrating the steps for the child and then allowing time for the child to repeat the steps using his or her own inventiveness. Having extra materials available allows for independent imagination and vision.

Although these projects are more specific, the themes in these activities are only suggestions; other ideas can be used. For instance, the 27 Fish Book might spark interest to make a three-part book on dragons or zoo animals, or the book can be turned vertically and the illustrations can be clowns where the head, body, and legs will be drawn in the three different sections.

After the child has formed the book and created the artwork, adults can encourage literacy development based on the skills of the child. Have the child tell a story or write nonfiction. Themes can be about family, people, animals, nature, sports, history, places, or things. Rhymes, songs, or poems by favorite authors can be inspiration, or a child can write his or her own original stories, songs, or poems. Alphabet or counting books are favorites for young children.

Flower Collage Book

Art Objectives and Techniques

Work with line, shape, and color
Create texture
Explore collage
Experiment with overlapping
Experiment with drawing technique
Experiment with cutting and pasting technique

Materials

- Simple Book (page 2)
- Magazines and/or catalogs with pictures of flowers
- Scissors
- Glue
- Crayons

Directions

→ View and discuss books about flowers.

→ Cut out pictures of flowers from the magazines. Glue them to both the front and the back covers, overlapping and filling in the entire sheet.

→ Use the crayons to draw pictures of flowers on each of the white pages.

Literacy Connection

Children can write descriptive sentences or a poem to go along with their drawings of flowers.

Swimming Fish Book

Art Objectives and Techniques

Work with line, shape, and color
Create movement
Create texture
Explore animation
Experiment with drawing technique

Materials

- Flip Book (page 3)
- White scrap paper
- Colored pencils
- Scissors

Directions

➜ View and discuss books on fish.

➜ View and discuss flip books and talk about animation.

➜ On scrap paper, draw the outline of a fish about 1 inch long and cut it out.

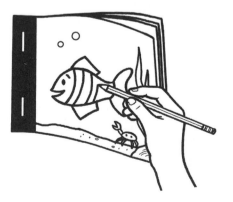

➜ On the last page of the Flip Book, trace the front part of the fish along one edge of the paper.

➜ On the next to last page, move the fish shape onto the page a little more and trace.

➜ Do the same thing on the next page, continuing to move the fish around the paper little bits at a time.

→ Color the fish in the same way on each page with colored pencils.

→ Draw a similar underwater scene on each page.

→ Flip the book from the back showing the last page first. The fish will move across the pages as if it is swimming.

Literacy Connection

Encourage children to tell or write a story about the fish illustrated in the book.

Under the Sea Book

Art Objectives and Techniques

Work with line, shape, and color
Create texture
Experiment with overlapping
Experiment with cutting and pasting technique
Experiment with drawing technique

Materials

- Half-Cover Book, not yet stapled together (page 4)
- Variety of colored construction paper scraps
- Scissors
- Glue
- Black fine-line marker
- Crayons
- Stapler

Directions

→ View and discuss books about sea life.

→ Talk about shapes, colors, and textures in the illustrations.

→ Design an underwater ocean scene on the front cover of the Half-Cover Book by cutting and pasting colored construction paper.

→ Design the top part of the book's inside back cover with something that would be above the water.

→ Color illustrations of an undersea story on some of the pages.

→ Write the story that was illustrated on other pages.

→ Staple the pages to the inside of the folded book in the order of the story.

Inspire children to draw pictures and write a story about the ocean and sea life.

Thumbprint Counting Book

Art Objectives and Techniques

Work with line, shape, and color
Create texture
Experiment with printing technique
Experiment with drawing technique

Materials

- Accordion-Fold Book (page 5) using 2 pieces of 6-by-24-inch white paper glued together
- Black ink pad
- Black fine-line marker
- Colored pencils

Directions

➜ View and discuss counting books.

➜ Demonstrate printing technique and how to make a thumbprint by pressing your thumb onto the ink pad and then pressing it onto a white page of the blank book.

➜ Discuss how the oval shape of the thumbprint can become various people, animals, or objects.

➜ On the first page of the Accordion-Fold book, make one thumb print. On the second page, make two thumbprints, make three on the third page, and so on, continuing until the last page.

➜ With the fine-line marker, make the thumbprints into the same thing on each page; for example, on page five, the prints could be made into five fish.

➔ Color the thumbprints in with colored pencils and draw a scene to go along with the colored prints.

➔ Write the number and a description of the thumbprints on each page, such as, "Five fancy fish swimming in the deep blue sea."

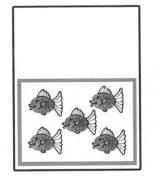

Literacy Connection

Descriptive number sentences can be written on each page instead of just label fragments.

 # City Book

Art Objectives and Techniques

Work with line and shape
Create texture
Work with horizontal and vertical lines
Experiment with overlapping
Create space
Experiment with cutting technique
Experiment with drawing technique

Materials

- Accordion-Fold Book (page 5) using 8-by-12-inch white paper, without front and back covers
- Scissors
- Black fine-line marker
- Crayons
- 1 piece of white paper
- Glue

Directions

→ View and discuss books about a city with large buildings. Talk about shapes and textures, and find horizontal and vertical lines.

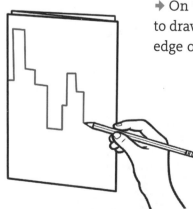

→ On the first rectangle, use the black fine-line marker to draw horizontal and vertical lines to make the contour edge of city buildings.

→ Cut around the top of the buildings, leaving the black marker line showing.

→ Add the windows, doors, and other details to the buildings with the marker.

→ On the second rectangle, draw horizontal and vertical lines for more buildings. The tops of these buildings should be taller than the buildings on the first page so that they show above the first buildings. Do not draw lower than halfway the height of the paper.

→ Cut the top edge of the second set of buildings and add the facade details.

→ On the last folded section draw clouds, the sun, birds, an airplane, or anything that would be in a city sky.

→ Color in with crayons.

→ Cut a piece of white paper the width of the last section and slightly below the height of the top edge of the second section's buildings, about 4 inches tall by 3½ inches wide.

The City
s large and noisy.
cars roar, and people
bout. Buildings are
her. Traffic is intense.
o navigate on foot.
perceived by tourists
que.

➡ Glue the paper to the last page, lined up with the bottom edge behind the buildings so that the paper will not show when the book is closed.

Literacy Connection

Encourage children to write a paragraph, story, or poem on the white paper about their experiences in a city.

Flower Collage Book

Under the Sea Book

Swimming Fish Book

One Circus elephant

Two tall giraffes

Four baby birds

Five fish ...

Six purple grapes

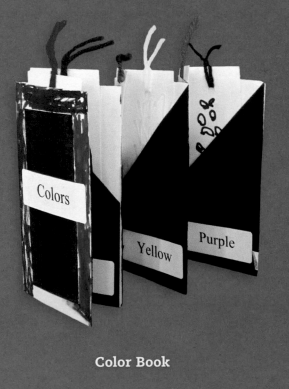

Colors

Yellow

Purple

Color Book

City Book

The City
...s large and noisy.
...cars roar, and people
...lly about. Buildings are
...er. Traffic is intense.
...d to navigate on foot.
...perceived by tourists
...ue.

Portrait Book

Alphabet Book

Chinese Treasures Book

27 Fish Book

Forest Stories Book

Snowman Book

Pop-Up Jungle Book

Mountain Majesty Book

Leaf Book

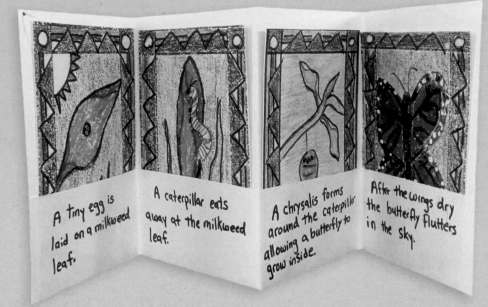

Inside the images: A tiny egg is laid on a milkweed leaf. A caterpillar eats away at the milkweed leaf. A chrysalis forms around the caterpillar allowing a butterfly to grow inside. After the wings dry the butterfly flutters in the sky.

Butterfly Life Cycle Book

Peek into the Ocean Book

Flapping Insects Book

Celestial Mobile Book

Pop-Up Creatures Book

Behold...
the
Dragons!

Mrs. Libby

Folding Dinosaurs Book

Creative Story Book

Watercolor Poetry Book

Color
Rythmn
Emphasis
Artistic
Texture
Energy

Red, yellow, and blue
I love to create
do you?

Paper, scissors, glue
Use them to see
what they do—

Color Book

Art Objectives and Techniques

Work with line, shape, and color
Create design
Explore pattern
Experiment with drawing technique

Materials

- Accordion-Fold Book (page 5), using 6-by-18-inch white paper, without front and back covers
- 7 pieces of black paper, 3 by 5 inches
- Glue
- Scissors
- 6 pieces of white paper, 2 by 5 inches
- Hole punch
- 3 pieces of yarn, one of each primary color (red, yellow, and blue), 4 inches long
- 3 pieces of yarn, one of each secondary color (green, orange, and purple), 4 inches long
- Markers in both primary and secondary colors
- White address labels

Directions

➜ View and discuss books on color. Talk about primary and secondary colors.

➜ Glue one piece of black paper to the middle of the cover page, leaving a white border around the edges.

➜ Vary the heights and looks of the other six pieces of black paper. For example, cut one black paper to 4 inches tall; cut one to 3 inches tall; tear one to 4 inches tall; fold the left corner of one black paper to the right edge and glue down; cut one black paper diagonally; fold one black paper down ¼ inch, fold again, and glue down.

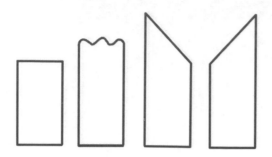

→ Glue three sides of each prepared black paper to each of the six white folded areas. Leave the top edge unglued, to make pockets.

→ Punch a hole in the tops of the six 2-by-5-inch white papers and tie a piece of colored yarn in each one.

→ Matching the color of the yarn, make a line design with a marker on each of the six pieces. Use one color per paper. Insert one into each pocket.

→ Attach a label to the pocket and write the color word that matches the colored bookmark.

→ On the cover, use all the colored markers to make a design in the white bordered edge.

→ Put a label with the word "Colors" on the front cover.

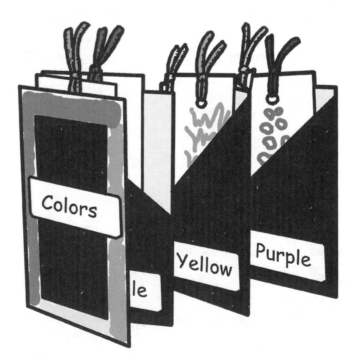

Allow children to read the color word and place the correct colored bookmark in the pocket. The bookmarks can be used to mark the child's place when reading other books. Find objects that are the particular colors of the bookmarks and list them. Write color poems.

Portrait Book

Work with line, shape, and color
Explore facial features
Explore proportion
Create texture
Experiment with drawing technique

Materials

- Accordion-Fold Book (page 5) using 6-by-24-inch white paper without the front and back covers
- Scissors
- Crayons

Directions

➔ View and discuss portraits, focusing on character faces in books.

➔ Discuss and practice making different facial expressions: sleepy, excited, frightened, happy, sad, bored. Talk about different hairstyles and how to make texture with line and color.

➔ Keep the Accordion-Fold Book folded, and round off all four corners with scissors to make an oval. The oval becomes the shape of the head.

➔ Draw different facial features and hairstyles on each oval with a black crayon, making details such as freckles, eyeglasses, and other individual traits.

➔ Color in the faces.

Literacy Connection

A story, song, or some descriptive sentences can be written about each person in the book. The book can be about friends, family members, community workers, or characters in a book.

Chinese Treasures Book

Art Objectives and Techniques

Work with line, shape, and color
Create texture
Explore collage
Experiment with overlapping
Experiment with cutting and pasting technique
Experiment with painting technique
Experiment with printing technique

Materials

- Coffee-Filter Pockets Book (page 7)
- Watercolor paints
- Photocopied Chinese characters
- Pencil
- Styrofoam to make a stamp of Chinese characters
- Stamp pad
- Small Chinese designs
- Tea bag or other small items relating to China
- Glue

Directions

➔ View and discuss books about Chinese culture.

➔ Decorate one coffee filter page of the Coffee-Filter Pockets Book with watercolor paints. Experiment with the flowing movement of the Chinese brush style.

➔ Decorate each of the coffee filters with different Chinese designs and prints. These can be hand-drawn, printed from a computer, or taken from papers preprinted with Chinese designs and lettering. Chinese restaurants often have paper covers for chopsticks that have designs or lettering on them, for example.

→ To make a stamp, draw Chinese letters in reverse on a thin piece of Styrofoam with a pencil, pressing the marks below the flat surface.

→ Glue a tea bag, or any other small objects that connect to Chinese culture, to the pages or place them in the pockets.

Literacy Connection

Children can use this book in connection with Chinese studies. Students might enjoy writing fortunes to place in the pockets. They can also write words, sentences, or stories and place them inside the filter pockets.

Alphabet Book

Art Objectives and Techniques

Work with line, shape, and color
Experiment with overlapping
Experiment with drawing technique

Materials

- Folded Book (page 8)
- Crayons and/or markers

Directions

→ View and discuss books about the letters in the alphabet.

→ Talk about how lines, shapes, and colors make designs.

→ On the cover of the Folded Book, write all the letters of the alphabet in random areas and sizes with black crayon or marker.

→ On each page of the book, draw four letters in various sizes and directions, in the order of the alphabet. Overlap and connect them to make various negative shapes. The back cover will have only two letters, Y and Z.

→ Choose three colors and color in the negative shapes created from the overlapping lines.

Encourage children to make a design with the letters of the alphabet. Play games by finding the different letters in the design and naming a word that begins with the particular letters.

27 Fish Book

Art Objectives and Techniques

Work with line, shape, and color
Create texture
Create pattern
Explore proportion
Experiment with drawing technique

Materials

- Three-Part Section Book (page 10)
- Black fine-line marker
- Crayons

Directions

➜ View and discuss some media about fish. Note the body parts and their proportions. Specifically point out the head, body, and tail.

➜ Talk about how line can make different textures to be used for scales, fins, and other features.

➜ With the black fine-line marker, draw a fish on the top paper of the Three-Part Section Book. Draw the head in the left-hand section, the body in the middle section, and the tail in the right-hand section.

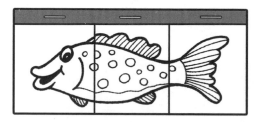

➜ Add smaller fish, weeds, or other water details.

→ Flip up the first paper section on the left-hand side and add a different head to the fish, making sure it connects to the body. Add underwater detail around the fish head. It should make sense with the previous drawing of the underwater environment.

→ Flip up the previously drawn fish body and draw the body of the second fish, making sure it attaches to the second head and the first tail in the correct places to show a smooth line from one part of the body to the others. Add the underwater details.

→ Flip up the first tail and draw the tail of the second fish and the underwater scenery.

➜ Repeat this process for a third fish on the last set of pages.

➜ Color in the top first fish to look like a complete fish with uniform colors.

➜ Flip up all three sections of the first fish, and color the second fish as a complete fish. Repeat for the third fish.

➜ When all three fish and their environments have been colored in, the different sections of paper can be flipped up at different levels to make mixed-up fish. The colors, details, patterns, and shapes within the fish will vary, but the bodies of the fish will look like a complete fish, fitting smoothly together.

Literacy Connection

Encourage children to write a poem, paragraph, or story about the fish illustrated in the book.

Forest Stories Book

Art Objectives and Techniques

Work with line, shape, and color
Create texture
Experiment with overlapping
Experiment with cutting and
pasting technique

Materials

- Portfolio Book (page 12), without
  fasteners
- Colored construction paper
- Scissors
- Glue

Directions

→ View and discuss books about the forest and the animals that live
there.

→ Using the colored construction paper, make objects found in a forest
scene, such as grass, trees, and animals. Glue them to both sides of the
outer cover of the Portfolio Book.

Literacy Connection

On the inside pages, encourage children to write a story about the forest
and the animals that live in the forest.

Snowman Book

Art Objectives and Techniques

Work with line, shape, and color
Create pattern
Experiment with drawing technique
Experiment with cutting and pasting technique

Materials

- Shaped Subject Book materials (page 14)
- Pencil
- White scrap paper
- Colored construction paper
- Scissors
- Glue
- Crayons (optional)

Directions

→ View and discuss books about snowmen.

→ Draw or trace three circles for a snowman on one piece of white paper. The top and bottom circles should touch the top and bottom of the paper.

→ Using the snowman template, follow directions for making the Shaped Subject Book to create a Snowman Book.

→ Cut out the shapes of a hat and scarf from colored construction paper. Glue them to the front cover. Add other clothing desired, such as a belt, jacket, vest, or buttons.

→ Add facial features to the snowman with construction paper or crayons.

Literacy Connection

Encourage children to write a story about a snowman on the inside pages.

Pop-Up Jungle Book

Art Objectives and Techniques

Work with line, shape, and color
Create texture
Create space
Explore relief
Experiment with cutting and pasting technique

Materials

- One-Fold Pop-Up Book (page 16)
- Blue paper, 4½ by 6 inches
- Green paper, 4½ by 6 inches
- Scissors
- Glue
- Variety of colored construction paper scraps
- Animal-print scrapbook paper (optional; it adds nice texture and patterns)

Directions

→ View and discuss books and artwork about a jungle or rainforest, including work by Henri Rousseau. Talk about shapes, colors, and textures.

→ Cover the top half of the One-Fold Pop-Up Book with the blue paper and the bottom half with the green paper.

→ With the colored construction paper scraps and animal-print paper, create a jungle scene. Glue some of the greenery and animals to the blue background and some to the green. Bend some of the cut shapes slightly on the bottom to create a tab. Glue the tab only, so that the pieces stand up independently.

➡ Glue the main character of your story to the front of the pop-up tab in the center.

Literacy Connection

Encourage children to write a story about a creature in a jungle or rainforest.

Mountain Majesty Book

Work with line, shape, and color
Create distance
Experiment with overlapping
Experiment with cutting and pasting technique

Materials

- Double-Sided Book (page 18)
- 2 pieces of purple construction paper in two shades, 6 by 11 inches
- Stapler
- Scissors
- Variety of colored construction paper scraps
- Glue
- Colored chalk or crayons
- 2 pieces of purple construction paper in two shades, 4½ by 5½ inches
- 1 piece of construction paper in a third purple or in pink or blue, 4½ by 5½ inches

Directions

➜ View and discuss books about mountains.

➜ Fold both 6-by-11-inch purple papers in half, short edge to short edge. Unfold the papers, stack them, and staple both papers at the crease to the inside of the first fold of the Double-Sided Book.

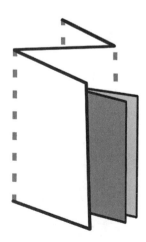

→ Create mountaintops with curved and jagged lines by cutting from the front edge of the first paper only to the fold. Cut the second paper a little higher than the first, and again only until the fold. This enables the reader to see all of the layers.

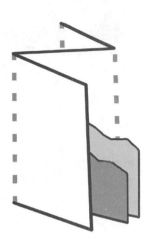

→ With colored construction paper scraps, add the night sky, such as a moon, clouds, and stars to the paper above the mountains.

→ Color a sky on the front cover with either colored chalk or crayons.

→ Cut the top edge of one of the 4½-by-5½-inch purple papers. On the other purple small paper, cut more mountain shapes, making sure the paper is shorter than the first cut paper. Repeat these cutting steps for the third small colored paper. When the papers are stacked, you should be able to see the mountaintops of each page.

→ Glue the mountain range stack to the front cover of the Double-Sided Book.

Literacy Connection

Encourage children to write a poem, paragraph, or story about mountains on the white interior pages.

 # Leaf Book

Art Objectives and Techniques

Work with line, shape, and color
Experiment with texture rubbing
Experiment with cutting and pasting technique

Materials

- Paper-Bag Pockets Book (page 19)
- Leaves
- 3 to 5 pieces of white paper (either 5 or 6½ inches square)
- Crayons
- Scissors
- Glue
- Optional: small stick and piece of yarn

Directions

➔ View and discuss books about leaves. Observe real leaves and note their textures and details.

➔ Make a texture rubbing of a leaf on each white paper by putting the leaf vein-side up underneath the paper and rubbing over the paper with the crayon until the entire leaf shows up.

➔ Cut out the leaves and glue one to each of the colored pages of the bag book.

➡ Poke a hole at the top and bottom of the spine. Tie the stick to the spine using yarn threaded through the holes.

Literacy Connection

Encourage children to write about leaves. An interesting story would be about the adventure of a leaf after it is blown off a tree. Place the stories, sentences, words, or poems inside the bag pockets.

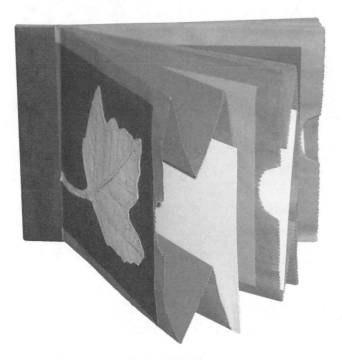

Butterfly Life Cycle Book

Art Objectives and Techniques

Work with line, shape, and color
Create pattern
Create texture
Explore symmetry
Experiment with drawing technique

Materials

- Folded-Pockets Book (page 21)
- 4 index cards, card stock, or white paper, 4 by 6 inches
- Ruler
- Black fine-line marker
- Crayons

Directions

→ View and discuss books about butterflies. Talk about the four stages of a butterfly's life cycle (egg, caterpillar, chrysalis, and butterfly).

→ On the four index cards or pieces of paper, draw a ½-inch border with the black marker. Draw a pattern inside the border and color in with crayon.

→ On each of the four cards, draw a picture illustrating one stage of the life cycle of the butterfly.

→ On the bottom fold of the pockets of the Folded-Pockets Book, write a sentence about the drawing in the pocket.

Prompt children to write sentences to go along with the life-cycle drawings.

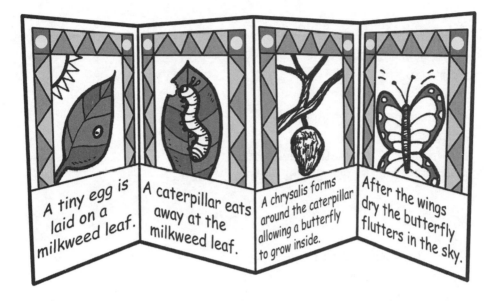

A tiny egg is laid on a milkweed leaf.

A caterpillar eats away at the milkweed leaf.

A chrysalis forms around the caterpillar allowing a butterfly to grow inside.

After the wings dry the butterfly flutters in the sky.

Celestial Mobile Book

Art Objectives and Techniques

Work with line, shape, and color
Create texture
Explore collage
Experiment with overlapping
Work with layering
Experiment with printing technique
Experiment with cutting and pasting technique

Materials

- Hanging Tassel Book (page 23)
- Rubber stamps of celestial objects
- Stamp pad
- Variety of paper scraps in white and warm colors (red, yellow, and orange)
- Shaped hole punch
- Variety of stars, sun, moon, and swirls cut from colored construction paper
- Scissors
- Glue

Directions

→ View and discuss books about the sky, both in daytime and nighttime.

→ View and discuss examples of mobile artworks.

→ Decorate the right-hand side of each section of a Hanging Tassel Book with stamped images, construction paper lines and shapes, and punched shapes with a celestial theme.

→ Attach celestial objects to the string, yarn, or ribbon tassel by tying or gluing them on.

Encourage children to write poems, words, or sentences with a celestial theme on the left-hand side of each section.

Peek into the Ocean Book

Art Objectives and Techniques

Work with line, shape, and color
Create texture
Create pattern
Experiment with overlapping
Experiment with cutting and pasting technique

Materials

- Tunnel Book (page 25), unassembled
- Blue paper, 5 by 6 inches
- Colored construction paper
- Scissors
- Glue

Directions

➜ View and discuss books about the ocean.

➜ Follow the directions on page 25 for making a Tunnel Book, up to the step for gluing the book together. This will be done after the pages are decorated.

➜ Glue the blue paper to the back solid rectangle.

➜ Cut out small fish, coral, seaweed, sea creatures, rocks, etc., from the colored construction paper.

➜ Glue some of your objects onto the blue paper to make an underwater scene.

➜ Glue other objects around the edges of the middle page with the cutout rectangle.

→ Glue more fish, underwater creatures, and underwater items to the front page with the cutout circle.

→ Now that the fish and underwater environments have been glued to the three pages, the solid blue page will be glued to the last folds, the decorated negative rectangle to the middle folds, and the decorated negative circle to the first folds, as described on page 26.

Literacy Connection

Inspire children to tell or write a story about life in the ocean.

Flapping Insects Book

Art Objectives and Techniques

Work with line, shape, and color
Create movement
Experiment with drawing technique
Experiment with cutting and pasting technique

Materials

- Flap Book (page 27)
- 12 pieces of white paper, 2 inches by 3 inches
- Black fine-line marker
- Colored pencils
- Scissors
- Glue
- Colored construction paper
- Pencil

Directions

→ Look at books about insects. Discuss the shapes, colors, patterns, and details of the insects.

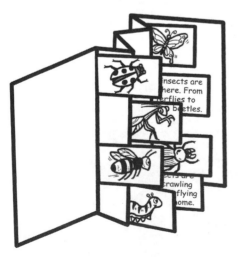

→ With the black fine-line marker, draw an insect a little smaller than 2 inches by 3 inches on a piece of white paper.

→ Color the insect in with colored pencils.

→ Cut out the colored insect and glue it to one of the flaps of the Flap Book.

→ Make another insect also a little smaller than 2 by 3 inches using colored construction paper, and glue it to a different flap.

→ Continue to make and glue down as many insects—both drawn and colored and cut out of paper—as there are flaps in the book.

→ Draw a large insect, 2½ by 8½ inches, on white paper with a pencil. Trace over the pencil line with the fine-line marker, color it in, and glue it onto the front cover.

Literacy Connection

Children can use this book in connection with studies about insects. Students can write up their research about insects on some of the flaps or make up imaginary bugs and write a story about them.

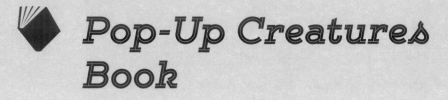

Pop-Up Creatures Book

Art Objectives and Techniques

Work with line, shape, and color
Create texture
Explore relief
Create facial expression
Experiment with layering
Experiment with cutting and pasting technique

Materials

- Pop-Up Book (page 29)
- Colored construction paper
- Scissors
- Glue

Directions

➤ View and discuss books with illustrations of dragons, monsters, aliens, or other creatures. Talk about the lines, shapes, colors, and textures in the illustrations.

➤ When making the two pop-ups from the directions for the Pop-Up Book (page 29), use the discussions of creatures to inspire the shape of the pop-ups.

➤ Cut and glue colored-paper facial features around the pop-up mouths and/or on their heads. Layer and overlap colors and shapes for the eyes, nose, hair, ears, horns, teeth, and any other details.

Encourage children to write about their creatures.

Folding Dinosaurs Book

Art Objectives and Techniques

Work with line, shape, and color
Create texture
Explore proportion
Create pattern
Experiment with drawing technique

Materials

- Mix-and-Match Book (page 31)
- Pencil
- Black fine-line marker
- Crayons

Directions

➜ View and discuss books on dinosaurs. Note the shapes and textures of the dinosaurs.

➜ Lay the inner squares of the Mix-and-Match Book flat. Using a pencil, draw a dinosaur on the top of the page with the head inside the left square and the body and tail in the square across from it. Trace over the pencil lines with the black fine-line marker, and color in with crayons.

→ Draw, trace, and color another dinosaur on the bottom part of the page with the head in the right square and body and tail in the left square.

→ Flip one of the squares and draw a different front or back of the dinosaur using other colors and patterns. Line up the lines between the head and the body.

→ Continue until all the squares have either a front or a back of a dinosaur on it.

→ Draw a dinosaur in its environment on the cover.

Literacy Connection

Inspire the children to write a sentence, paragraph, story, or poem about dinosaurs.

Watercolor Poetry Book

Art Objectives and Techniques

Work with line, shape, and color
Investigate color mixing
Create texture
Experiment with painting technique

Materials

- Three-Cover Book (page 33)
- Watercolor paints
- Paintbrushes
- Black fine-line marker or pen

Directions

➡ View and discuss poetry books.

➡ Paint the middle section of a Three-Cover Book with watercolors.

→ Use the end sections for writing poems that relate to the watercolor images.

Literacy Connection

Students can write poems to express the feelings inspired by the paintings, not just the literal paintings.

Creative Story Book

Art Objectives and Techniques

Work with line, shape, and color
Experiment with detail
Experiment with drawing technique

Materials

- Stitched Book (page 35)
- Pencil
- Crayons

Directions

→ Read and discuss a short story, talking about the characters and setting. Note the beginning, middle, and end of the story.

→ Brainstorm ideas and let the students create their own stories with illustrations and text using pencil and crayons.

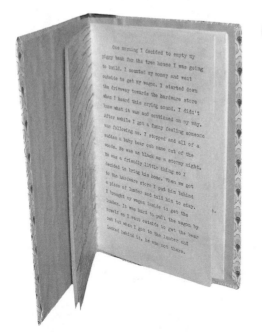

Literacy Connection

Encourage children to write a creative short story about something that interests them.

Conclusion

Art enhances imagination, creativity, and self-esteem, yet the value it holds in academic development is too often overlooked. Art encourages learning through problem solving, cognition, and critical thinking. I have always felt that art is basic to education and should be considered the fourth *R*, as necessary a course of study as reading, writing, and arithmetic.

Along with sensory motor skills, art develops social, emotional, cognitive, and complex thinking skills. Through art children develop skills sequentially and progress in abilities that range from simple to complex. Various art materials can provide development of different skills through exploration and learning.

Art activities promote literacy and language development, expressive as well as reflective skills, visual literacy, and verbal creativity. Reading comprehension improves when children are involved in art-related activities connected to the stories they read. They also become excited and eager to read or write about new material. Children love art because it is enjoyable. By linking art with literacy, children will find reading and writing enjoyable.

Besides the impact that art has on individual children, art is important across the curriculum. Literacy is directly affected by the art process of organizing content and composition. The process of the art activity itself, not just the end product, is important to learning. The encouragement of teachers and parents in facilitating art activities is invaluable in facilitating learning. Art activities can and should be used to create a rich literacy environment.

Making books provides a fun opportunity for children to develop language. Children become engaged in the activity of making their own books and using descriptive words to discuss their creations. When expressing themselves, they develop a sense of innovation. Bookmaking encourages the process of creativity as well as strengthens the experience of thinking and communicating.

Glossary

accordion fold paper folded in a series of back-and-forth folds or zigzag fashion that resembles the bellows of an accordion

acrostic composition where the first letters of each line are aligned vertically to form a word

adventure story story that presents the unknown or unexpected with features of danger, excitement, and risk

aesthetic appreciation of the beauty in art or nature

alliteration repetition of the initial consonant sounds of words in a phrase

art appreciation awareness of the aesthetic values in artwork

art medium materials used to create artwork

background the part of a piece of art that looks farther away or is behind other parts

balance the arrangement of visual elements so that the parts seem to be equally important

basic shapes circle, square, triangle, and rectangle

bind the process of joining pages together

blank book a formed book with no text or illustration

body the main part of the text

characterization manner in which an author develops characters and their personalities

cinquain a stanza of five lines with successive lines of two, four, six, eight, and two syllables

cityscape a view or picture of a city

collage artwork made by assembling and gluing materials to a flat surface

composition the arrangement of design elements into proper relation

construct to create artwork by putting materials together

contour the outline of a shape or form

contrast a great difference between two things

cool colors colors that remind people of cool things; they often create a calm or sad feeling: blue, green, and purple

cover paper paper used for the outside covers

crayon rubbing placing a textured paper or shape under another paper and rubbing the top paper with crayon to show the texture of the bottom paper or shape

creative having the ability to make things in a new or different way

design the ordered arrangement of art elements in a piece of art

design elements the basic tools an artist works with: line, shape, form, color, value, and texture

design principles the way an artist uses the design elements: unity, balance, rhythm, movement, variety, repetition

drawing describing something by means of line

emphasis special stress of one or more design components

endpapers the papers that are glued to the inside of the covers of a book

fable a story with a teaching theme or moral, usually with animal characters

fantasy a story about the unreal, with events that may be magical or supernatural

figurative language language that represents one thing in terms of something dissimilar: simile, metaphor, personification, hyperbole, symbol

flap book a book where flat pieces of paper are attached to the book by one side only so that they can swing back and forth

flip book a book where pages are moved quickly to animate the drawing on the pages

foreground the part of a piece of art that seems near or close

form a three-dimensional design

free form a free-flowing, imaginative shape or process

genre type or category to which a literary work belongs

geometric shapes shapes that have smooth edges

gutter the middle of the book between the spread

horizontal a line that goes from side to side

illustration any picture, diagram, or non-text item in a book

imagery language that appeals to the five senses

landscape artwork that shows an outdoor scene

limerick humorous verse with five lines in the rhyme pattern of aabba

line a mark made by a moving point

margin the space between the edge of the page and the printed text

metaphor an implied comparison between dissimilar objects

mixed media artwork made up of different materials or techniques

motif a recurring feature of a literary work that is related to the theme

movement the rhythmic qualities of a design

narrative a story that generally includes character, setting, plot, and theme

negative space empty space in a design

nonfiction prose that explains or describes reality

nonobjective a style of art where the main ideas or feelings come from the design, created with colors, lines, and shapes; it does not show objects or scenes

original artwork that looks very different from other artwork; a new idea

overlap one part that covers some of another part

pattern lines, colors, or shapes repeated in a planned way; a model or guide for making something

perspective artwork in which the shapes of objects and distances between them look realistic

picture book a book in which the illustrations are as important or even more important than the words in telling the story

plot the sequence of events in a literary work

poetry a literary work with rhythmical composition; verse

pop-up part of a book that comes away from the flat pages when the pages are opened

portrait artwork that shows the face of a person

positive space the actual shapes or figures in a design

primary colors colors from which other colors can be made: red, blue, and yellow

print to press something with ink or paint on it to create an image

proportion the size, location, or amount of something as compared to something else

realism a style of artwork that shows objects or scenes as they look in everyday life

relief something that stands out from a flat background

repetition the repeated use of the same design elements

rhythm a repetition of design elements to create a visual balance

scoring scratching or making a slight incision that allows for a smooth fold

secondary colors colors made from primary colors: purple, green, orange

shape book a book with a form or appearance to resemble a specific object

space an empty place or area

spine the edge part of the book that connects the two covers together and holds the book's pages together

spread two pages that face each other

stanza a group of lines forming a unit in a poem

stencil a flat material with a cutout design

style an artist's own way of creating art

symmetry parts arranged the same way on both sides

tall tale impossible or exaggerated happenings related in a
humorous way

technique a special way to create artwork

texture the way something feels or the way it looks like it feels

theme the underlying main idea of a literary work

tunnel book pages bound with two folded strips on each side and
viewed through an opening in the cover. Each page has an opening to
allow the viewer to see through the entire book to the back, creating
a dimensional scene inside.

two-dimensional artwork that is flat and measured in two ways,
height and width

unity the quality of having all parts look as if they belong

value the lightness or darkness of a color

vertical a line that runs up and down

warm colors colors that remind people of warm things: red,
yellow, orange

Suggested Reading

Animation by Patrick Jenkins (Addison-Wesley, 1991)

The Big Book of Picture-Book Authors & Illustrators by James Preller (Scholastic Professional Books, 2001)

A Book of One's Own by Paul Johnson (Heinemann, 1998)

How a Book Is Made by Aliki (HarperCollins, 1988)

How to Make Books with Children by Joy Evans and Jo Ellen Moore (Evan-Moor Publication, 1985)

How to Make Pop-Ups by Joan Irvine (Beech Tree Books, 1991)

The Literacy Dictionary: The Vocabulary of Reading and Writing by Theodore L. Harris and Richard E. Hodges (International Reading Association, 1995)

Literature-Based Art Activities by Darlene Ritter (Creative Teaching Press, 1991)

Making Books by Charlotte Stowell (Kingfisher Books, 1994)

Multicultural Books to Make and Share by Susan Kapuscinski Gaylord (Scholastic Trade, 1999)

Round-the-World Folktale Mini-Books by Maria Fleming (Scholastic, 1999)

Storytime Crafts by Kathryn Totten (Upstart Books, 1998)

Teaching Art with Books Kids Love by Darcie Clark Frohardt (Fulcrum Publishing, 1999)

Using Caldecotts Across the Curriculum by Joan Novelli (Scholastic Professional Books, 1999)

Using Stories to Make Art: Creative Activities Using Children's Literature by Wendy M. L. Libby (Cengage Learning, 2004)

The Young Author's Do-It-Yourself Book by Donna Guthrie, Nancy Bentley, and Katy Keck Arnsteen (Millbrook Press, 1994)